FC BARCELONA

MORE THAN A CLUB

Abbeville Press Publishers

New York · London

A portion of the book's proceeds are donated to the **Hugo Bustamante AYSO Playership Fund,** a national scholarship program to help ensure that no child misses the chance to play AYSO Soccer. Donations cover the cost of registration and a uniform for a child in need.

Text by Illugi Jökulsson

For the original edition
Design and layout: Ólafur Gunnar Guðlaugsson

For the English-language edition
Editor: Joan Strasbaugh
Production manager: Louise Kurtz
Designer: Ada Rodriguez
Copy editor: Ken Samuelson

PHOTOGRAPHY CREDITS

Getty Images
24–25 Koeman: David Cannon. 32–33 Messi and Van der Sar: Shaun Botterill. 34–35 Goal: Shaun Botterill. 42–43 Messi and Eiður Smári: Jasper Juinen. 45 Rivaldo: Clive Brunskill.

Shutterstock
2, 3, 8, 9, 10, 11, 16, 17, 20, 21, 22, 23, 28, 29, 36, 37, 38, 39, 40, 41, 48, 49, 50, 51, 52, 53, 54, 55, 56, 57, 58, 59.

Images from FC Barcelona
12–13 Old images: Photographer unknown/Archive FCB. 14 César Rodriguez: Photographer unknown/FC Barcelona Archives. 44 Maradona: Seguí/FC Barcelona. 44 Ronaldo: Seguí/FC Barcelona. 18–19 Cruyff: Seguí/FC Barcelona.

This book is published in association with **FC Barcelona.**

All statistics current through the 2012–2013 season unless otherwise noted.

First published in the United States of America in 2014 by Abbeville Press, 137 Varick Street, New York, NY 10013

First published in Iceland in 2012 by Sögur útgáfa, Fákafen 9, 108 Reykjavík, Iceland

First edition
10 9 8 7 6 5 4 3 2 1

Library of Congress Cataloging-in-Publication Data

Illugi Jvkulsson.
  FC Barcelona : more than a club / Illugi Jvkulsson.—First edition.
    pages cm— (World soccer legends)
  ISBN 978-0-7892-1158-3 (hardback)—ISBN 0-7892-1158-0 (hardcover) 1. Futbol Club Barcelona—History—Juvenile literature. I. Title.
  GV943.6.B3I45 2014
  796.334'64094672--dc23
                    2013045839

For bulk and premium sales and for text adoption procedures, write to Customer Service Manager, Abbeville Press, 137 Varick Street, New York, NY 10013, or call 1-800-ARTBOOK.

Visit Abbeville Press online at **www.abbeville.com.**

CONTENTS

CATALONIA

Spain is divided into several regions and Catalonia is one of them. Catalonia is an autonomous community whose main spoken language, *Catalan*, is related to the most widespread language of Spain, *Castilian*, or *Spanish*. You will find some Catalan words in Barça's story.

The flag of Spain

The flag of Catalonia

Catalonia covers an area that is slightly smaller than the state of Connecticut. But while Connecticut has just 306 million people, Catalania has 7.5 million. (The total population of Spain is 48 million.) Barcelona is the capital of Catalonia and the largest city by far, with a population of 1.6 million.

LARGEST CITIES IN SPAIN

	City	Population
1.	Madrid	3.2 million
2.	Barcelona	1.6 million
3.	Valencia	800,000
4.	Seville	700,000
5.	Zaragoza	675,000
6.	Málaga	570,000
7.	Murcia	430,000
8.	Palma, Mallorca	400,000
9.	Las Palmas	380,000
10.	Bilbao	355,000

Barcelona faces the Mediterranean.

FAMOUS CATALANS

In the 19th century, Catalonia became the hub of industry in Spain. Its inhabitants are known for their strong work ethic and diligence. Art, culture, and sports have always been held in high esteem. Joan Miró and Salvador Dalí were among the most innovative painters of the 20th century, and the architect Antoni Gaudí designed very unique buildings.

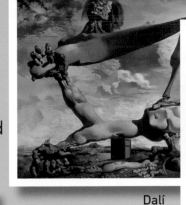

Dalí

Miró

Gaudí

DID THE CATALANS COME FROM SWEDEN?

In the first centuries BC, a tough nomadic tribe called the Goths lived in Sweden. The Goths migrated far and wide and played their part in the fall of the Roman Empire in the 5th century AD. At some point, the Goths were joined by a tribe from Iran called the Alans. The Goths and Alans finally settled in Spain, and the area they occupied was called Goth-Alania. In time that changed to Gothalania and finally into Catalonia. Well, that's at least one theory to explain the name Catalonia. Another theory is that it originally meant "Land of Castles."

Europe around AD 450

SWEDEN
GOTLAND
Migration of the Goths
POLAND
UKRAINE
ROMAN EMPIRE
SPAIN
Migration of the Goths ITALY
Migration of the Alans
Mediterranean

It's worth noting that not everyone agrees with this theory about Catalonia's name.

BARCELONA

The area around Barcelona has been inhabited for a very long time. Some believe that the city's name comes from Hannibal Barça, the great general from Carthage, in North Africa, who ruled Spain for some time. He waged war against the Romans in the 3rd century BC and almost won. This explanation is, however, quite unlikely.

Barcelona expanded rapidly in the 19th century. Business was booming, and industry attracted people to the city. The newcomers were appreciated and the atmosphere was liberal. Beautiful buildings popped up at great speed, and the city became famous for its vibrant and colorful culture. These trends continued into the 20th century.

Everyone who comes to Barcelona should visit the highly unusual and striking Sagrada Familia church. It was designed by the architect Antoni Gaudí (1852–1926).

AN IMMIGRANT FROM SWITZERLAND

Among those drawn by the charms of Barcelona was a young man from Switzerland named Hans Gamper. He arrived in 1898 intending to stay only for a short while, but he was so fascinated by the city that he lived out the rest of his days in Barcelona.

Gamper, whose first name became Joan after he settled in Barcelona, was passionate about sport, especially soccer. The game had started to spread through Europe from England only a few decades before, and it was known and played by very few in Spain. Gamper wanted to change that. On October 22, 1899, he placed an ad in a local sports magazine asking if there were any men in the city interested in establishing a soccer club.

Joan Gamper (1877–1930)

The advertisement

11

The Barcelona team in 1903

THE BIRTH OF BARÇA

Eleven men turned up at the meeting Joan Gamper called in October 1899 and they became the founding members of Futbol Club Barcelona. Gamper himself, a passionate striker, played on the team the first four years and scored over 100 goals in 48 games! He and his teammates were obviously a force to be reckoned with, and they won the first trophy for the club in 1902. That was in the Copa Macaya tournament, which would later become the Championship of Catalonia and finally the Copa Catalunya. So even in its early days the club was already one of the strongest in Spain.

Yet there was trouble these first years. For a while the club was verging on bankruptcy until the accountant Gamper took over the books, as well as scoring goals! He got the club back on track. Barcelona won several trophies, and in 1910 it won the Copa del Rey (the Spanish Cup) for the first time.

It was around this time that the club took up Catalan instead of Castilian as its official language. The club gradually became a symbol of Catalan identity and the life and soul of the Catalan struggle for self-determination.

The Spanish league—La Liga—was founded in 1929. Barcelona had already won the Copa del Rey eight times, and now added the first Liga title to its collection of silverware. In second place was a club that was fast becoming Barcelona's "favorite rival"—Real Madrid.

The next fifteen years were tough on Barça. For several seasons, the club had trouble landing any trophies, and from 1936 to 1939

Spain was ravaged by a civil war that ended with the dictator General Francisco Franco seizing power. Franco was opposed to all expressions of Catalan self-governance, and was therefore against the main symbol of Catalan identity—FC Barcelona. Slowly but surely, however, the club regained its former glory, and in 1945 Barcelona was once again crowned champion.

THE FIRST SUPERSTAR

Paulino Alcántara was born in 1896 in the Philippines, where his Spanish father served in the military. His mother was a local. The family moved to Barcelona the same year that FC Barcelona was founded, and Joan Gamper recruited the young Alcántara to the team. He was only fifteen years old when he debuted for the team and scored a hat trick. He was an unstoppable scorer, and his shots were so powerful that he once tore a hole in the netting of the opponents' goal. Another time, a police officer accidentally got in the way of Alcántara's shot, and both the officer and the ball landed in the netting.

Paulino Alcántara
1896–1964
Played for Barcelona 1912–1916 and 1918–1927
Matches 357
Goals 369
Internationals for Spain 5
Goals 6

Albert

The original crest of Barcelona. The current crest, which can be found on page 15, is based on a design by Carles Comamalas, who won a competition held by the club. He was on the team and was a doctor by trade.

The second-largest football club in Barcelona is called Espanyol. It was founded in 1900 and has always been the "small club" in Barcelona. Espanyol has never won La Liga, but it has claimed the Copa del Rey four times. The atmosphere tends to be quite boisterous when Barça and Espanyol meet on the field.

Aside from Paulino Alcántara, Josep "José" Samitier was Barça's most celebrated scorer in the early decades. He was with Barça 1919–32, played 454 matches, and scored 333 goals. After a dispute with Barcelona's management he transferred to Real Madrid but didn't play very much for the club. He returned to Barça as a coach and led the club to a championship in 1944–1945.

César Rodriguez
1920–1995
With Barcelona 1939–55
Matches 351
Goals 232
Internationals for Spain 12
Goals 6

MÉS QUE UN CLUB

Barcelona won La Liga, the top league in Spain, four times over the six-year period from 1948 to 1953. Around this time Barça was not simply a symbol of the Catalan struggle for self-determination, but also a token of silent opposition to the country's dictator, Franco, who had seized power after the Civil War. FC Barcelona was therefore more than a club—*més que un club*.

At this time, the key player in Barça's front line was César Rodriguez. This brilliant forward held the record for goals scored for decades to come. Luis Suárez was another great goal-scoring Spaniard on the team who played for the club from 1954 to 1961, scoring 114 goals. Barcelona native Antoni Ramallets stood guard in the goal from 1948 to 1962.

Some of the club's key players came

from abroad. In 1951, Ladislao—or László—Kubala, a refugee from Hungary, joined Barça. He was an all-around striker with a great eye for passing and a fantastic scorer. Kubala was without doubt one of the world's best players in the '50s. Toward the end of that decade, two more refugees from Hungary joined the club: Sándor Kocsis and Zoltán Czibor, who had both played for the renowned Hungarian national team, just like Ferenc Puskás of Real Madrid. The Hungarians were part of the highly successful Barça team that won La Liga with brilliant offensive play in two consecutive years, 1959 and 1960. There were of course other fine players on the team, most notably the Brazilian Evaristo de Macedo.

László Kubala
1927–2002
Played with Barcelona 1951–61
Matches 345
Goals 274
Internationals for Czechoslovakia, Hungary, and Spain 28
Goals 15

DREAMS OF EUROPEAN GLORY

Barça's greatest ambition was to win the European Cup, which its rival Real Madrid had completely dominated during the competition's first five years, with Puskás and Di Stéfano as their best players. In the 1959–1960 season Barça lost to Real in the semifinals. But the following year, when Spain's archrivals again faced each other in the semifinals, Barcelona knocked the five-time champions out. Barça then made it all the way to the final but rather unexpectedly lost to the Portuguese club Benfica, a new powerhouse in European football. This seemed to dampen spirits within Barça, and the club hit a long slump despite having recently opened a splendid new stadium at Camp Nou.

Sándor Kocsis played 235 matches for Barça and scored 151 goals.

CAMP NOU

FC Barcelona's first home ground was Camp de la Indústria, or L'Escopidura. It had a capacity of around 6,000 and was considered quite well equipped at the time. But the club soon outgrew it, so in 1922 a new and impressive stadium called Camp de Les Corts was constructed. At first it held 20,000 spectators, but after several expansions it could accommodate 60,000 people. With time, even Les Corts became too small for the club, and in 1957 Camp Nou was opened, less than one mile away from the old stadium.

In the beginning Camp Nou could hold 106,146 spectators, but when Spain hosted the 1982 World Cup, the stadium was expanded to hold 121,749. As improvements were made to the facilities, the old standing area was abolished, and currently the stadium has room for 99,354 people. There are plans to expand again in the near future.

Camp Nou is the largest soccer stadium in Europe. The second-largest is Wembley (90,000) in England and the third, Santiago Bernabéu in Madrid (85,000). The largest stadium in the world is in North Korea, holding over 150,000 people. India, Mexico, and Iran also have stadiums that are larger than Camp Nou.

Camp Nou is almost invariably sold out, and the atmosphere is thrilling.

A NEW ERA

Barcelona won the Copa del Rey three times between 1963 and 1971, but the club was less successful in La Liga. In 1973, the management decided to use every available means to change that, and bought the Dutch player Johan Cruyff from Ajax in Amsterdam. At the time Cruyff was widely regarded as the best and smartest soccer player in the world, a worthy successor to the Brazilian genius Pelé.

Cruyff was the leader and greatest player of a fantastic Dutch national team, where passing and skill had replaced force and physical strength. This type of soccer suited Barcelona. Cruyff scored quite a few devious goals, but it was his vision and uncanny ability to time passes that made him a superior player. His most famous goal was the "Phantom Goal," when he scored by turning in midair and volleying the ball, which had traveled wide off the far post, into Atlético Madrid's net with his right heel.

Barça had bet on the right horse. The club became Spanish champions in 1974, and their beautiful attacking play won over soccer enthusiasts in Spain and abroad. But despite the club's popularity, several fantastic players, and some impressive victories, it couldn't seem to break the spell of bad luck in La Liga in the long run. When Johan Cruyff left Barça in 1978, he gave the new club president, Josep Lluís Núñez, some sound advice: "Establish a youth academy. That will bring you success." And that's just what Núñez did. The academy became world famous under the name of La Masia.

Cruyff's goal against Atlético was dubbed the Phantom Goal, because it was almost spooky how he managed to reach the ball and volley it into the net. Just take a look on YouTube!

Johan Cruyff
b. 1947
With Barcelona 1973–1978
Matches 227
Goals 83
Internationals for the Netherlands 48
Goals 33

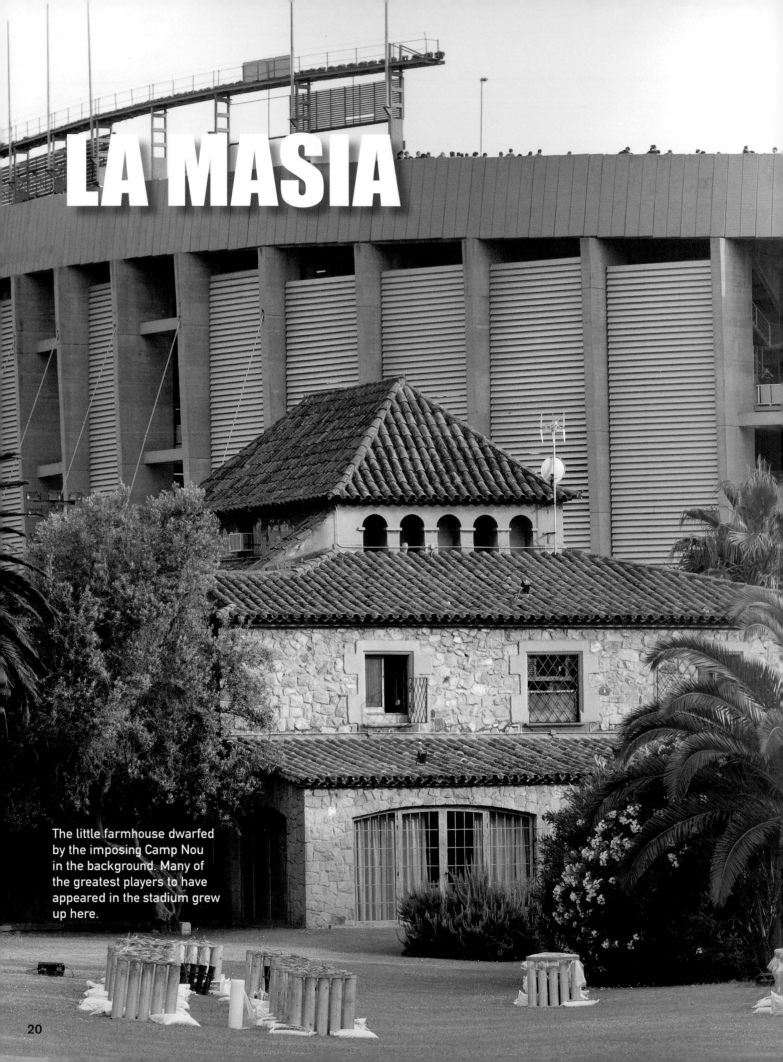

LA MASIA

The little farmhouse dwarfed by the imposing Camp Nou in the background. Many of the greatest players to have appeared in the stadium grew up here.

La Masia simply means "the Farmhouse," and the building dates back to 1702, when it was a country residence outside of the city. The club bought it in 1954, during the construction of the new Camp Nou stadium next to it. La Masia originally housed the club's offices, but in 1979 it was turned into the headquarters and training facility of Barça's recently established youth academy. Hence La Masia became the symbol of this powerful, well-organized, and successful youth program, and of the impressive soccer that Barcelona has played for the past twenty or thirty years.

Some of the most promising talents lived in the La Masia dormitory, and on the club's training grounds they learned the short and accurate passing and moving that have become the Barça philosophy. Even though Barça continued to buy great players from other clubs, it was the club's official policy to build the team primarily with young players raised in La Masia. This was how Barcelona finally became more successful than its rival Real Madrid, which followed the so-called Galácticos policy, buying world-famous players each year and trying to mesh them together into a successful team.

Pep Guardiola, Guillermo Amor, Albert Ferrer, and Sergi Barjuán are all La Masia alumni, and they were key players in the very successful Barça team of the 1990s. The beginning of the 21st century saw an even greater generation emerge from the academy: Xavi, Iniesta, Messi, Busquets, Piqué, Pedro, and Fàbregas.

By 2011, the youth academy had outgrown the old building, and the young players moved to a new modern facility. But the philosophy and principles of Barça's youth academy will continue to be synonymous with the name La Masia.

CALLING CRUYFF

Barcelona won La Liga in the 1984–1985 season. It was the team's tenth title, but 11 years had passed since the last one. The club had, however, won a few good trophies in other tournaments during that time, including the 1979 Cup Winners' Cup, which Barça won 4–3 against Fortuna Düsseldorf with goals from Tente Sánchez, Juan Asensi, Carles Rexach, and Hans Krankl. Barça regained the same title in 1982, beating Standard Liège 2–1 with goals from the diminutive Dane Allan Simonsen and Quini, who was the club's leading scorer at the time.

After the tenth La Liga victory, there were high hopes that the club was back on track towards another golden era. The team played well under the leadership of its German captain Bernd Schuster, but things took a turn for the worse in the European Cup in 1985–1986. Barcelona just scraped through to the final by beating Swedish club Göteborg in a penalty shoot-out, after having lost the first game 3–0. And then the Catalan club lost the final to the Romanian club Steaua Bucharest after another penalty shoot-out. The club was also losing ground in La Liga, so Barça then turned to the man who had helped them rise from the ashes before, Johan Cruyff. In May 1988, he took over as coach.

THE DREAM TEAM

Under Cruyff's management, Barça rose to unprecedented heights. They won their first trophy in 1989, when Barça defeated Sampdoria from Italy 2–0 in the Cup Winners' Cup final. Three years later, they met again in the European Cup final, which you can read about on pages 24–25.

In the spring of 1990, Barça won a sweet victory over Real Madrid in the Copa del Rey final, and then famously won La Liga four consecutive times—a club record that still stands.

Not only did Barça win a host of titles under Cruyff's guidance, but the club also played a truly beautiful brand of soccer and was often referred to as the "Dream Team."

There were several contributing factors. Cruyff recruited international stars, such as his countryman Ronald Koeman, the relentless striker Hristo Stoichkov of Bulgaria, the elegant Michael Laudrup from Denmark, and the highly gifted Brazilian Romário. Established players from other Spanish teams also arrived, especially Basques: Jose Mari Bakero, Txiki Begiristain, Julio Salinas, and—last

but not least—the incredible goalkeeper Andoni Zubizarreta. He was in fact already on the team when Cruyff took over, and he played a total of 490 matches from 1986 to 1994. But the core of Cruyff's Dream Team was increasingly made up of La Masia players.

By May 1996, Barça had won eleven titles and trophies under Cruyff. He left them that month but has maintained a strong bond with Barcelona ever since.

Even with Cruyff gone, the Dream Team made a huge impact on the club. Barça had now become accustomed to winning and would no longer accept extended periods without silverware. Furthermore, the foundations had been laid for the spectacular style of soccer that Barcelona has played ever since.

The "Dutch connection" also endured for years. In 1997, Louis van Gaal from the Netherlands took over as coach and delivered two consecutive La Liga victories, in 1997–1998 and 1998–1999. Several strong Dutch players played for the team at the turn of the new century: defenders Frank de Boer, Michael Reiziger, and later Giovanni van Bronckhorst; midfielder Phillip Cocu; and striker Patrick Kluivert.

A LONG-AWAITED VICTORY!

The Dream Team was almost knocked out of the 1991–1992 European Cup by the German club Kaiserslautern in the second round, but then made it quite convincingly to the final against Sampdoria. The Italian club was one of the strongest teams in their country at the time, and boasted strong attackers such as Gianluca Vialli and Roberto Mancini, who later became coach of Inter Milan, Manchester City, and, currently, Galatsaray. Two years earlier, Barça had beaten Sampdoria easily 2–0 in the European Cup Winners' Cup, but this time the Italians were tougher and defended well against Barça's superb strikers. Each team made several attempts, but the ball just wouldn't go into the net. With only 8 minutes to spare in extra time, Barça was awarded a free kick just outside the penalty area and defender Koeman finally thrust the ball into the net. Barcelona had at long last won the coveted European Cup! Celebrations broke out among the blaugrana fans: the Dream Team had finally made their dream come true.

Koeman was ecstatic after scoring his fabulous goal.

1992 was a great year in sports for Barcelona: the city also hosted the Olympics, which were considered a triumph and enhanced the city's reputation.

1

European Cup

May 20, 1992
Wembley, London, UK

BARCELONA – SAMPDORIA

1–0

Koeman 112

Zubizarreta

Ferrer – Nando – Koeman – Juan Carlos

Bakero – Sacristán – Guardiola (Alexanko 113) – Stoichkov

Michael Laudrup – Salinas (Goikoetxea 64)

BLAUGRANA

Blue and scarlet have been Barcelona's colors from the very outset. In Spain, they are referred to as *blaugrana*, which simply means "blue-garnet" in Catalan. Various tones of blue and red stripes have been used, as can be seen below.

There are a few stories about how Barça came to choose these colors. For a long time, the prevailing explanation was that Joan Gamper had brought these colors with him from Switzerland where his football team was supposed to have played in them. This has, however, turned out to be wrong.

Another popular theory is that Gamper, who was an accountant, was inspired by the colors of the pencils he used for work. But there seems to be little truth to this explanation, either.

Yet another theory is that one of Barça's first players, the Englishman Arthur Witty, had worn these colors when he played for Crosby's Merchant Taylors' School back in Liverpool, and brought his uniform with him.

But whatever the truth is, the blue and scarlet are now recognized worldwide, and several soccer clubs now use them as their official colors.

There are several soccer clubs called Barcelona in countries all over the world, such as Brazil and in Cape Verde. The most famous Barcelona club outside of Catalonia is a strong team in the Ecuadorian top division. It uses the FC Barcelona crest almost unaltered, but doesn't play in the blaugrana. The reason is that shortly after the club was founded in 1925 it lost several consecutive matches in the blaugrana, and the club president swore that the team would never play in those colors again. Barcelona SC in Ecuador thus plays in yellow shirts and black shorts.

1950

1960

1970

1980–92

1999–2000

2001–2

2003–4

2008–9

2010–11

2012–13

ONWARD AND UPWARD

After the spring of 1999, Barcelona didn't win a single trophy or title for five years. There were some excellent players on the team who continued to play admirable soccer, but the titles seemed out of reach.

Yet another Dutchman, Frank Rijkaard, changed that. He came to Barcelona as head coach in the summer of 2003 and in his second season the titles started pouring in. Barça won La Liga in both 2004–2005 and 2005–2006 and with spectacular play, seized the Champions League title for the second time in 2006.

Barça's number-one player during this time was without a shadow of doubt, the Brazilian wizard Ronaldinho. When he was in his prime, there was no one who could match him in tricks, skill, and pure strokes of genius. The front line also boasted the incredible scorer Samuel Eto'o, from Cameroon. The Portuguese Deco dominated the midfield together with the increasingly impressive homegrown talent, Xavi. And on defense a player from northern Catalonia, Carles Puyol reigned supreme with his lion's mane. He is a true leader on the field and became captain in 2004.

In October 2004, Rijkaard gave a seventeen-year-old from Argentina , Lionel Messi, his first shot at La Liga.

After a few years of success, Barça failed to win significant trophies, and Rijkaard left in the summer of 2008. The new manager was a former midfield anchor and captain of Barcelona, Pep Guardiola.

Ronaldinho was twice voted best player in the world while he was with Barcelona.

Ronaldinho
b. 1980
With Barcelona 2003–8
Matches 250
Goals 110
Internationals for Brazil 97
Goals 33

Barcelona relied increasingly on tiki-taka, its short pass-and-move style of soccer. Tiki-taka also became more noticeable in the way the national team played as more young Barça players joined the roster. It proved very successful, and since 2008 the Spanish have been almost unbeatable in international tournaments.

Samuel Eto'o
b. 1981
With Barcelona 2004–9
Matches 232
Goals 152
Internationals for
Cameroon 112
Goals 55

Frank Rijkaard

Carles Puyol
b. 1978
Debuted 1999
Matches 581
Goals 16
Internationals for Spain 100
Goals 3

EUROPE AT THEIR FEET

Barcelona won its second Champions League title in 2006, when the team overcame Arsenal in Paris.

This was a match to watch. Barcelona had just been crowned Spanish champions, and the virtuosos in the front line seemed to be able to score at will. The Catalans had already knocked out Chelsea, Benfica, and AC Milan on the road to the final. But Arsenal was a force to be reckoned with, beating both Real Madrid and Juventus. The match was formidable: even though their goalkeeper was sent off in the 18th minute of the first half, Arsenal managed to score and seemed to keep up with Barça well into the second half of the game. Then Barça increased the pace of attack, and Frank Rijkaard brought out his secret weapon—the Swedish striker Henrik Larsson. He entered the game, provided Eto'o with an assist for the equalizer, and a few minutes later set up the winning goal by another sub, Juliano Belletti. Barça won its second European title, in the first year after the Champions League took over from the European Cup.

The Brazilian defender Juliano Belletti played for Barça for three years. The winning goal in the 2006 UEFA Champions League was the only goal he ever scored for the club.

Captain Puyol with the trophy

UEFA Champions League

May 17, 2006
Stade de France, Paris, France

BARCELONA – ARSENAL

2–1

Eto'o 76   *Campbell 37*
Belletti 81

Valdés

Oleguer (Belletti 71) – Márquez – Puyol – Van Bronckhorst

Edmilson (Iniesta 46) – Deco – Van Bommel (Larsson 61)

Giuly – Eto'o – Ronaldinho

THE THIRD EUROPEAN TITLE

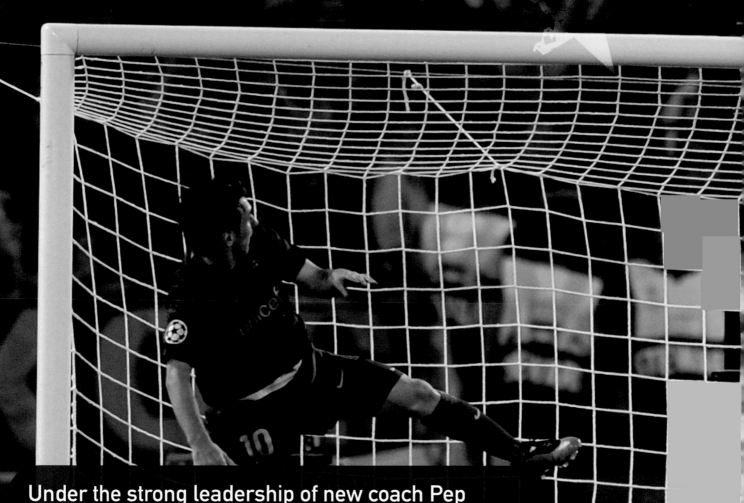

Under the strong leadership of new coach Pep Guardiola, Barcelona breezed through the group stage of the Champions League. The team then beat the French club Lyon in exciting matches in the round of 16, and knocked Bayern Munich out in the quarterfinals with surprising ease. In the semifinals, however, Barça ran into trouble against a very determined Chelsea. In a home game at Camp Nou, Barça seemed to be headed out of the Champions League, having not had a shot at the goal for 93 minutes. But then Iniesta scored, and Barça went through to the final.

It was a different Barça that showed up for the final against Manchester United in Rome. United started with a bang, but after 10 minutes Barcelona took charge of the game and never looked back. Eto'o scored a fine goal, and then Messi sealed the victory with a rare header after an assist from Xavi. The renowned Cristiano Ronaldo didn't manage to deliver in his last match for Manchester United.

3

UEFA Champions League

May 27, 2009
Stadio Olimpico, Rome, Italy

BARCELONA – MAN. UNITED

2–0

Eto'o 10
Messi 70

Valdés

Puyol – Yaya Touré – Piqué – Sylvinho

Xavi – Busquets – Iniesta (Pedro 92)

Messi – Eto'o – Henry (Keita 72)

It came as no surprise that Messi scored, but no one expected him to score with a header. United's goalkeeper, Edwin van der Sar, seemed totally flabbergasted.

33

THE FOURTH!

Barça defeated Manchester United in the Champions League final—again!

Barcelona easily won its group in the group stage of the 2010–2011 Champions League season. The Catalan club then knocked out Arsenal in the round of 16, and went on to effortlessly beat Shakhtar Donetsk from the Ukraine in the quarterfinals. Barça faced its archrival Real Madrid in the semifinals and knocked them out without much trouble, Messi scoring two goals in an away game in Santiago Bernabéu. In the final at Wembley against Manchester United, Barcelona's superiority was even more evident than it had been two years earlier. United tried their best and managed to hold their own for a time, but in the end they were completely outplayed by the brilliant tiki-taka game of Barcelona.

4

UEFA Champions League

May 28, 2011
Wembley Stadium, London, UK

BARCELONA – MAN. UNITED

3–1

Pedro 27   *Rooney 34*
Messi 54
Villa 69

Valdés

Alves (Puyol 88) – Mascherano – Piqué – Abidal

Xavi – Busquets – Iniesta

Pedro (Afellay 92) – Messi – Villa (Keita 86)

Edwin van der Sar watches the ball land in the net as Pedro scores the opening goal. Messi was also ready to pounce!

EL CLÁSICO

See "Ten Facts" on pages 58–59

Barcelona and Real Madrid are the two great empires of Spanish soccer, and when these two rivals meet spirits run high, both on the field and in the stands. Their matches are called "Clásicos" because they tend to be epic and become instant classics. They are usually a spectacle of passionate and extremely competitive soccer.

The two clubs have a remarkably equal share of victories and defeats. Real was the stronger side in the past, but Barça's success in the past years has more or less evened the score.

Matches 1916–Summer 2013	224
Barça victories	86
Real victories	90
Draws	48
Goals Barça–Real	361–378

The most goals scored in draws were in the Copa del Rey 1916 (6–6), and La Liga 1943 (5–5).

Three memorable recent Barça victories in El Clásico

November 19, 2005
Barcelona 3
Eto'o 15, Ronaldinho 60, 78
Real Madrid 0

Ronaldinho

Real's lineup was a star-studded Galácticos team: Iker Casillas, Roberto Carlos, Zinedine Zidane, Ronaldo, David Beckham, Robinho, Raúl. Barcelona had Xavi and Deco in midfield, and the eighteen-year-old Messi up front. Messi showed his true talents by setting up the first goal for Samuel Eto'o. The brightest star of the match, however, was Ronaldinho who was magical and scored 2 goals. His performance was so impressive that he received a standing ovation in Santiago Bernabeu—a very rare occurrence in the heated Clásicos.

May 2, 2009
Barcelona 6
Henry 17, 58, Puyol 19, Messi 35, 75, Piqué 83
Real Madrid 2
Higuaín 14, Ramos 56

Thierry Henry

One of Barça's most glorious victories under Guardiola's guidance. Real scored the first goal, but it didn't seem to have any effect on Barça other than to spur them on to take full control of the match. Xavi and Iniesta were in their very best form, dazzling with their passing skills, and Messi proved that he was probably already the best player in the world. And Thierry Henry played his best game in the blaugrana shirt. Real put up a good fight to begin with but was crushed by the superior Barça, which ended up with three trophies that spring—La Liga, the Copa del Rey, and the Champions League.

Xavi

November 29, 2010

Barcelona 5

Xavi 10, Pedro 18, Villa 55, 58, Jeffrén 91

Real Madrid 0

Real, under the guidance of José Mourinho and boasting the talents of Cristiano Ronaldo, had a great start in La Liga but was given a lesson in tiki-taka soccer by Guardiola's wonder team. Barça held possession of the ball with short, accurate passes. It was appropriate that the grandmaster of this style, Xavi, scored the first goal. The only surprise of the game was that Messi didn't score despite playing beautifully. After the beating, Mourinho admitted that his team had been outclassed by Barcelona.

5 CONSECUTIVE VICTORIES

From 1962 to 1965, Real won 6 consecutive Clásicos in La Liga. Barça almost equaled that record by winning 5 consecutive victories between December 13, 2008, and November 29, 2010. In these 5 matches, Barça scored 16 goals while only conceding 2. Messi scored 4, Pedro, Villa, and Thierry Henry 2 each, and Eto'o, Xavi, Puyol, Piqué, Zlatan Ibrahimovic, and Jeffrén 1 each. In the 6th match, Messi scored a goal for Barça, and the game stood 1–0 until Cristiano Ronaldo scored an equalizer from the penalty spot in the 82nd minute.

BARÇA'S GREATEST VICTORIES

September 24, 1950

Barcelona 7 Real Madrid 2

Nicolau 9, 56, César Rodriguez 14, Marcos Aureli 39, 88, Marià Gonzalvo 62, Basora 82, Molowny 15, García González 66

April 21, 1935

Barcelona 5 Real Madrid 0

Martí Vantolrà 43, 62, 68, 82, Escolà 48

March 25, 1945

Barcelona 5 Real Madrid 0

César Rodriguez 41, 46, Bravo 52, Escolà 77, Marià Gonzalvo 86

February 17, 1974

Barcelona 5 Real Madrid 0

Asensi 30, 54, Johan Cruyff 39, Juan Carlos 65, Sotil 69

January 8, 1994

Barcelona 5 Real Madrid 0

Romário 24, 56, 81, Koeman 47, Iván Iglesias 86

Then there was the victory on November 29, 2010, also 5–0.

MESSI, THE TOP SCORER

Lionel Messi has scored more goals in official matches against Real than any other Barça player. At the end of the 2012–13 season, he had scored a total of 18 goals in these matches. Next came César Rodriguez, with 14 goals. Alfredo di Stéfano holds the Real record, which is also 18 goals, scored between 1953 and 1964. Messi should have plenty of time to improve the record and put it beyond the reach of others!

Lionel Messi

GUARDIOLA!

Pep Guardiola was only thirty-seven years old when he took over as head coach of Barcelona in the summer of 2008. He was raised in La Masia and was a virtuoso of the elegant playing style called tiki-taka. Under his management this method was developed to such perfection that even the most formidable adversaries only managed about 30–35% possession. The wizards of Barcelona always seemed to find a teammate, often toying with their opponents for great lengths of time before a devastating pass or a lightning-quick run ended with a goal. Even though Guardiola was very mild mannered and almost reserved, he inspired his team, and many believe that Barcelona under his management was the best soccer team of all time. The titles and trophies were stacked up, and Guardiola was certainly Barça's most successful coach. He resigned in 2012 due to fatigue, and was replaced by his assistant Tito Vilanova, who made Barcelona champions in 2012–13, when the team reached 100 points in La Liga! Sadly, Vilanova then had to resign in the summer of 2013 because of serious illness. Argentine coach Gerardo Martino was hired to take over.

Josep Guardiola
b. 1971
Played for FCB 1990–2001
Matches 472
Goals 10
Internationals for Spain 47
Goals 5
Coach, FCB 2008–2012,
Matches 247
Victories 179
Draws 47
Defeats 21

Martino

Vilanova

BARCELONA TROPHIES AND TITLES UNDER GUARDIOLA'S MANAGEMENT

2008–2009

La Liga	1st place (87 points)
Copa del Rey	Won
Spanish Super Cup	Won
UEFA Super Cup	Won
UEFA Champions League	Won
FIFA Club World Cup	Won

2009–2010

La Liga	1st place (99 points)
Spanish Super Cup	Won

2010–2011

La Liga	1st place (96 points)
Spanish Super Cup	Won
UEFA Super Cup	Won
UEFA Champions League	Won
FIFA Club World Cup	Won

2011–2012

La Liga	2nd place (91 points)
Copa del Rey	Won

There was a great atmosphere within Barça under Guardiola's management, which isn't surprising—there was a lot to be happy about!

GOALS GALORE

Barcelona lost the Liga title to their archrivals Real Madrid in the 2011–2012 season. The blow was softened slightly by the fact that Barça's best player, the genius Lionel Messi, broke all goal-scoring records during the season. In Barcelona's 60 matches in 2011–12, Messi scored a whopping total of 73 goals, which was a world record for one season.

Messi scored goals in all six tournaments that Barcelona took part in: La Liga, the Spanish Cup, the Spanish Super Cup, the UEFA Champions League, the European Super Cup, and the FIFA Club World Cup.

MESSI GOALS	Matches	Goals
La Liga	37	50
Champions League	11	14
Spanish Cup	7	3
Other matches	5	6
Total	60	73

In addition, Messi scored 9 goals for the Argentinian national team during the season.

MESSI!

Messi scored a hat trick against Getafe in La Liga on March 20, 2012, becoming Barça's top scorer in official games. The record was formerly held by César Rodriguez, who scored 232 goals from 1939 to 1955.

On March 7, 2012, Messi scored 5 goals in the Champions League against Bayer Leverkusen. No player had managed that since the European Cup was replaced by the Champions League in 1992.

Messi scored 10 hat tricks for Barcelona during the 2011–12 season, 8 in La Liga and 2 in the Champions League.

An Incredible Record!

In 2012, Messi broke the record for goals scored in one year, previously held by the German Gerd Müller, who had scored a total of 85 goals in 1972. Messi scored 91 goals in 2012, 79 for Barcelona and 12 for Argentina. He scored his 79 goals for Barcelona in just 60 matches!

Spectators in Camp Nou applaud the Ballon d'Or awarded to Messi in 2011. His teammates join in. Messi has always stressed that without them he wouldn't enjoy the success he does.

STARS IN THE BLAUGRANA

Maradona

Many of the best players in the world have joined Barcelona, although some of them didn't stay long.

DI STEFÁNO

Alfredo di Stefáno, undoubtedly one of the very best strikers of all time, was born in Argentina in 1926. Di Stéfano was about to sign a contract with Barcelona in 1953 and even had his picture taken in the Barça shirt. But through complicated machinations, Real Madrid managed to "steal" him, and he scored over 300 goals for the Madrid club during the next decade.

MARADONA

Diego Maradona was a member of the Barcelona team for two seasons, 1982–84. He played 73 matches and scored 45 goals, but injuries and disputes with the club's management cast a shadow on his stay with Barça. He transferred to Napoli in Italy, and in 1986 he played a pivotal role in securing the World Championship title for the Argentinian national team.

RONALDO

The Brazilian Ronaldo was just twenty years old when he came to Barça in 1996, but he had already been nominated Player of the Year by FIFA. He scored the winning goal in Barça's 4th victory in the Cup Winner's Cup on May 14, 1997. With his strength and lightning speed he scored a ton of goals, a total of 47 in 49 matches. His most famous goal was against Compostela in La Liga—take a look on YouTube! Unfortunately, Ronaldo got into disputes with the club management and left rather abruptly. He would return to Camp Nou later on—but wearing the Real Madrid colors!

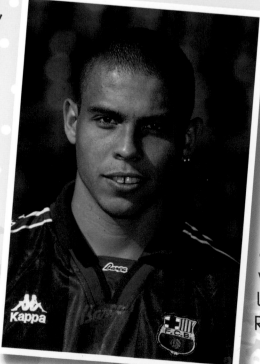

Ronaldo

Rivaldo
b. 1972
With Barcelona 1997–2002
Matches 235
Goals 136
Internationals for Brazil 74
Goals 34

RIVALDO

Rivaldo from Brazil played for Barcelona for five very successful years, 1997–2002, twice becoming Spanish champion with the club. He will always be remembered for his outstanding performance in the last match of the 2000–2001 season, when Barça had to defeat Valencia in order to win a Champions League place. Rivaldo scored a hat trick in Barça's 3–2 victory, and his unforgettable third goal was a glorious overhead kick from the edge of the box in the final minutes of the match at Camp Nou.

Barça's Victories
in La Liga, Spanish Cup, and the European Cup/UEFA Champions League

	Winners	La Liga	Copa del Rey*
1929	Barcelona	Champions 1	
1929–30	Bilbao	2nd place	
1930–31	Bilbao	4th place	
1931–32	Real Madrid	3rd place	
1932–33	Real Madrid	4th place	
1933–34	Bilbao	9th place	
1934–35	Real Betis	6th place	
1935–36	Bilbao	5th place	
1939–40	Atlético Madrid	9th place	
1940–41	Atlético Madrid	4th place	
1941–42	Valencia	12th place	Cup 9
1942–43	Bilbao	3rd place	
1943–44	Valencia	6th place	
1944–45	Barcelona	Champions 2	
1945–46	Sevilla	2nd place	
1946–47	Valencia	4th place	
1947–48	Barcelona	Champions 3	
1948–49	Barcelona	Champions 4	
1949–50	Atlético Madrid	5th place	
1950–51	Atlético Madrid	4th place	Cup 10
1951–52	Barcelona	Champions 5	Cup 11
1952–53	Barcelona	Champions 6	Cup 12
1953–54	Real Madrid	2nd place	
1954–55	Real Madrid	2nd place	
1955–56	Bilbao	2nd place	
1956–57	Real Madrid	3rd place	Cup 13
1957–58	Real Madrid	3rd place	
1958–59	Barcelona	Champions 7	Cup 14
1959–60	Barcelona	Champions 8	
1960–61	Real Madrid	4th place	
1961–62	Real Madrid	2nd place	
1962–63	Real Madrid	6th place	Cup 15
1963–64	Real Madrid	2nd place	
1964–65	Real Madrid	6th place	
1965–66	Atlético Madrid	3rd place	
1966–67	Real Madrid	2nd place	
1967–68	Real Madrid	2nd place	Cup 16
1968–69	Real Madrid	3rd place	
1969–70	Atlético Madrid	5th place	
1970–71	Valencia	2nd place	Cup 17
1971–72	Real Madrid	3rd place	
1972–73	Atlético Madrid	2nd place	

Josep Samitier, one of Barça's greatest from 1919–32, nicknamed "el Mag" or "the Magician."

César Rodriguez, Barça's second player to become top goal scorer in Spain, 1948–49.

Ladislao Kubala played with Barça for a decade, 1951–61, and scored a total of 274 goals.

	Winners	La Liga	Copa del Rey*	Europe
1973–74	Barcelona	Champions 9		
1974–75	Real Madrid	3rd place		
1975–76	Real Madrid	2nd place		
1976–77	Atlético Madrid	2nd place		
1977–78	Real Madrid	2nd place	Cup 18	
1978–79	Real Madrid	5th place		
1979–80	Real Madrid	4th place		
1980–81	Real Sociedad	5th place	Cup 19	
1981–82	Real Sociedad	2nd place		
1982–83	Bilbao	4th place	Cup 20	
1983–84	Bilbao	3rd place		
1984–85	Barcelona	Champions 10		
1985–86	Real Madrid	2nd place		
1986–87	Real Madrid	2nd place		
1987–88	Real Madrid	6th place	Cup 21	
1988–89	Real Madrid	2nd place		
1989–90	Real Madrid	3rd place	Cup 22	
1990–91	Barcelona	Champions 11		
1991–92	Barcelona	Champions 12		1
1992–93	Barcelona	Champions 13		
1993–94	Barcelona	Champions 14		
1994–95	Real Madrid	4th place		
1995–96	Atlético Madrid	3rd place		
1996–97	Real Madrid	2nd place	Cup 23	
1997–98	Barcelona	Champions 15	Cup 24	
1998–99	Barcelona	Champions 16		
1999–00	Deportivo Coruna	2nd place		
2000–01	Real Madrid	4th place		
2001–02	Valencia	4th place		
2002–03	Real Madrid	6th place		
2003–04	Valencia	2nd place		
2004–05	Barcelona	Champions 17		
2005–06	Barcelona	Champions 18		2
2006–07	Real Madrid	2nd place		
2007–08	Real Madrid	3rd place		
2008–09	Barcelona	Champions 19	Cup 25	3
2009–10	Barcelona	Champions 20		
2010–11	Barcelona	Champions 21		4
2011–12	Real Madrid	2nd place	Cup 26	
2012–13	Barcelona	Champions 22		

Sándor Kocsis, the amazing Hungarian, was among Barça's top scorers from 1958 to 1966.

Andoni Zubizarreta was Barça's goalkeeper from 1986 to 1994 and won several awards.

* Before La Liga was established in 1929, the Spanish Cup (known as the Copa del Rey) was the main tournament in Spain. Barcelona had won the trophy 8 times in those first decades: 1910, 1912, 1913, 1920, 1922, 1925, 1926, and 1928.

NEYMAR

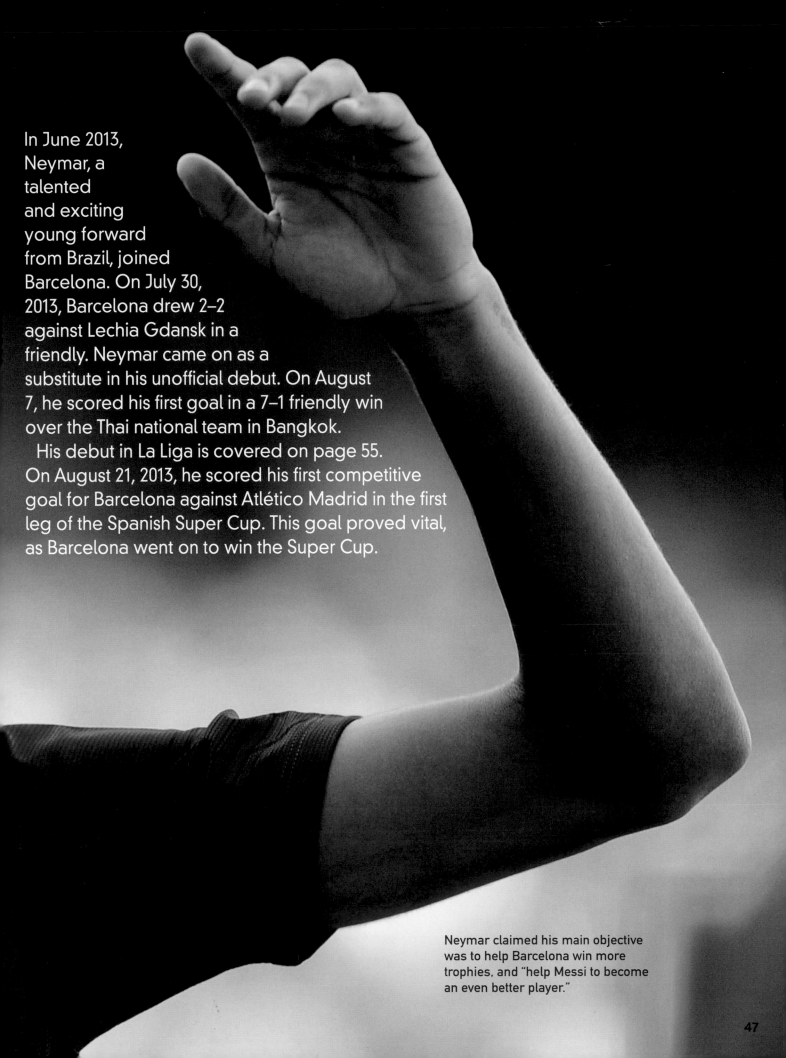

In June 2013, Neymar, a talented and exciting young forward from Brazil, joined Barcelona. On July 30, 2013, Barcelona drew 2–2 against Lechia Gdansk in a friendly. Neymar came on as a substitute in his unofficial debut. On August 7, he scored his first goal in a 7–1 friendly win over the Thai national team in Bangkok.

His debut in La Liga is covered on page 55. On August 21, 2013, he scored his first competitive goal for Barcelona against Atlético Madrid in the first leg of the Spanish Super Cup. This goal proved vital, as Barcelona went on to win the Super Cup.

Neymar claimed his main objective was to help Barcelona win more trophies, and "help Messi to become an even better player."

Messi

Lionel Andrés Messi was born on June 24, 1987, in the city of Rosario, Argentina. He was shy and modest but showed incredible talent at a very early age. The only problem was that he suffered from growth-hormone deficiency, which meant that without medical treatment he wouldn't grow beyond four foot eight. His parents couldn't afford the treatment and Messi's future in soccer was uncertain, to say the least. However, at the age of thirteen, he was invited for a trial with Barcelona. It took the head coach at the time, Carles Rexach, just a few minutes to realize that this boy was an extraordinary talent. The young Messi signed with the club, which agreed to foot his medical bills so that he could reach his full height. Messi has been playing brilliantly for Barcelona ever since. He is considered one of the very greatest players of all time.

Messi's first official match for Barça was on October 16, 2004. He came on as a substitute in a Liga match against the second-largest club in Barcelona, Espanyol.

When Messi points to the sky after scoring, he is honoring the memory of his grandmother Celia. They were very close, and she took him to football practice when he was a child.

MESSI
b. 1987
Debuted in 2004
Matches 379
Goals 313
Internationals for Argentina 82
Goals 35

Messi started the 2013–2014 season of La Liga by scoring 5 goals in his first 2 games!

Messi the wizard is the only player to have scored 5 goals in a Champions League game.

No Spanish player has received as many awards and trophies as Xavi, either with Barcelona or the Spanish national team.

Xavi

Javier Hernández i Creus was born on January 25, 1980, on the outskirts of Barcelona. His father was a player with the Catalan team Sabadell. Xavi started playing for Barça's youth teams at the age of eleven, and showed great promise early on. He was eighteen when he debuted with the first team in the 1998 Spanish Super Cup, in which he scored Barça's only goal in a defeat against Mallorca. But Xavi has not often been on the losing side. He took over from Pep Guardiola as Barcelona's principal playmaker, and soon proved that he was a true genius on the field.

He has incredible ball control, and his passes are nothing short of remarkable—they almost always find a teammate. After Xavi was paired up with Iniesta, Barça's midfield has simply been the best in the world. And Xavi controls the center field like an omniscient orchestra conductor. The key to his success, he claims, is that he's constantly looking for spaces to pass the ball to. When Messi joined the team, always ready to receive passes from Xavi or Iniesta and drive the ball between the goalposts, Barça became almost invincible. Fans worry that they will have to wait a long time for someone who can fill Xavi's shoes. But as of 2013, he shows no signs of slowing down.

Xavi regularly scores spectacular goals. He had his most prolific season in 2011–2012, when he scored 14 times in all competitions.

A legendary Clásico game between Barcelona and Real took place on Real's home ground on May 2, 2009. Xavi was at his majestic best as Barcelona won 6–2. He didn't score himself, but racked up four assists, for Puyol, Thierry Henry, and Messi (twice).

Xavi
b. 1980
Debuted 1998
Matches 677
Goals 80
Internationals for Spain 126
Goals 11

Iniesta

INIESTA
b. 1984
Debuted 2002
Matches 455
Goals 47
Internationals for
Spain 87
Goals 11

Andrés Iniesta Luján was born in a small village in the province of Albacete in Spain. The nearest city was Valencia. At the age of twelve, his soccer talents and skills got him into Barcelona's La Masia youth academy. He claims to have cried his eyes out when he left home, and he's always been a modest, down-to-earth guy who is fond of his roots. Because of these traits, Iniesta kept a low profile, but he was soon to become one of the vital parts in the tiki-taka machine that made Barça the most entertaining and successful club in the world.

His midfield interplay with Xavi is legendary. They always seem to know where the other is. Alex Ferguson, Manchester United's former manager, claims that Iniesta is Barça's most lethal player. "He's fantastic. He makes the team work. The way he finds passes, his movement and ability to create space is incredible." In 2012, Iniesta won the UEFA Best Player in Europe Award, ahead of his teammate Lionel Messi and Real Madrid's Cristiano Ronaldo.

One of the many nicknames Iniesta has in Spain is "El Caballero Pálido" (The Pale Rider) on account of his pale complexion.

In view of his incredible skill, Iniesta has sometimes been "accused" of not scoring enough goals. Yet he has scored some very important goals in his career, both for Barça and the Spanish national team. He scored the winning goal against the Netherlands in South Africa in 2010, when the Spanish finally became world champions.

When Iniesta scored the winning goal at the 2010 World Cup, he took off his jersey to reveal the writing on his shirt: *Dani Jarque: siempre con nosotros* which means "Dani Jarque: always with us." Dani was Iniesta's friend, teammate on Spain's U-21 national team, and captain of the Espanyol team. He had died from a heart attack the year before.

Valdés
Born 1982
Debuted in 2002
Matches 501
Internationals
for Spain 16

Busquets
Born 1988
Debuted in 2008
Matches 236
Goals 8
Internationals for
Spain 59
No goals yet

THE FIVE MUSKETEERS!

Víctor Valdés i Arribas was born on January 14, 1982, and has been with Barça since he started playing soccer. He has broken every goalkeeping record there is for the club, and stood between the posts in more matches than the famous Andoni Zubizarreta. At first, he was sometimes accused of being reckless and inconsistent, but in truth he is as solid as they come. He has won the Zamora Trophy a record 5 times. He plans to transfer to another club in the summer of 2014, but is expected to stand guard in Barça's goal until then.

Sergio Busquets Burgos was born on July 16, 1988. One reason that the great midfielders and strikers of the front line can have such a free rein is that deeper in the midfield Barça has strong players, quick to regain possession if the opponents are on the break. The lanky Busquets is the latest addition to this guard. He might not seem as accomplished as Xavi, Iniesta, and Messi, but he plays his very important role with increasing confidence, and is very good at keeping the ball in play. Busquets has been a regular with the Spanish national team for some time.

Fàbregas
Born 1987
With Barça since 2011
Matches 99
Goals 29
Internationals for Spain 83
Goals 13

Piqué
Born 1987
With Barça since 2008
Matches 228
Goals 16
Internationals for Spain 57
Goals 4

Neymar
Born 1992
With Barça since 2013
Internationals for Brazil 39
Goals 24

Francesc or "Cesc" Fàbregas Soler was born on May 4, 1987, in a small town just outside Barcelona. He joined La Masia at a very early age. In 2003, he took the surprising step of joining Arsenal and starting his career there. He spent eight very successful years with the London club and developed into an all-around attacking midfielder. In 2011, he realized his dream of returning to Camp Nou, where he is expected eventually to take over from Xavi, which is no surprise, given his ability to pass with pinpoint accuracy.

Gerard Piqué i Bernabeu was born on February 2, 1987, in Barcelona. He grew up within the club and played with Messi and Fàbregas on La Masia's youth teams.

He left the club at an early age, just like Fàbregas, and went to Manchester United. But he returned to Camp Nou and is a worthy heir to Puyol's position in defense. Piqué is a bit more adventurous and enjoys playing out of defense and running forward into an attack.

Neymar arrives
For years, speculation had been rife at Camp Nou about the arrival of Brazilian wunderkind Neymar, and he finally showed up during the summer of 2013. Neymar is blessed with exceptional pace, dribbling skills, and clinical finishing. He debuted in La Liga when Barcelona mauled Levante 7–0 on August 18, 2013. He came on for Alexis Sánchez in the 63rd minute.

THE NEXT GENERATION

La Masia continues to breed extraordinary players by the dozen. Some of the young men below might very well become the next Camp Nou legends.

Deulofeu 1994

Gerard Deulofeu Lázaro was born on March 13, 1994, in the village of Riudardenes in Girona Province, in the far north of Catalonia. He joined the youth academy at the age of nine, and in the autumn of 2011 he joined Barcelona B, in Spain's second division. He did very well there, and soon word about his exceptional abilities as a forward began to spread. He likes to play as a striker or an attacking right winger. In October 2012, he played for the senior team for the first time. In July 2013, he went on a season-long loan to the English club Everton to gain the experience necessary to harness his great talent.

Tello 1991

Cristian Tello Herrera was born on August 11, 1991, in the town of Sabadell in Catalonia. He started his professional career with Espanyol but joined Barça in 2010 to play with Barcelona B. In the autumn of 2011, he was called up for the first team and got to play quite a bit. He scored 2 goals, for instance, in a famous 7–1 victory over Bayer Leverkusen in the Champions League in March 2012. Lionel Messi scored the other 5 goals. Tello is quick on his feet and a skilled forward or left winger. In August 2013, Tello played his first international for Spain, a friendly against Ecuador.

Dongou 1995

Jean Marie Dongou Tsafack, or simply Dongou, is a quick and skillful yet powerful striker from Cameroon who had been plying his trade with Barça B, but played his first game for the main team on August 2, 2013. He took part in the Joan Gamper Cup final and scored a goal.

Sergi Roberto 1992

Sergi Roberto Carnicer was born on February 7, 1992, in Reus in the wine region of Catalonia. He is well on his way to winning a place on the first team. Sergi Roberto is a versatile attack-minded midfielder who can play most positions in the center of the field.

Cuenca 1991

Joan Isaac Cuenca López was born on April 27, 1991, in Reus, like Sergi Roberto. He is another of the attack-minded wingers whom Barcelona seems to produce in droves. He played a bit for the first team but then went on loan to AFC Ajax.

TEN FACTS

FC Barcelona fans are often called *Los culés,* which translates into "The Asses." This nickname can be traced back to when the club played its home games at the Camp de la Indústria. There were no stands, so the fans would sit up on the wall that surrounded the field while watching the game. Passersby couldn't help but see a long row of backsides—the Asses! Even though the club has come a long way since then—and, in fact, has the largest stadium in Europe—the name stuck.

One of the La Masia players doing well with Barça's first team lately is the scorer Pedro Rodríguez Ledesma. He was born in 1987 in Tenerife in the Canary Islands. During the 2009–2010 season, he accomplished the remarkable feat of scoring a goal in six different official competitions that Barcelona took part in. Two years later Lionel Messi repeated the feat.

Barcelona is owned by its thousands of supporters. No single billionaire can buy the club. The club president is elected directly by all the owners-supporters. Josep Lluís Núñez was the longest-serving president, from 1978 to 2000. Joan Laporta was president during the very successful period between 2003 and 2010, and currently the position is held by Sandro Rosell.

Barça and Real have never met as often in a short period of time as in the spring of 2011. In 18 days, the clubs played 4 Clásicos. On April 16, the teams drew at Santiago Bernabeu in La Liga, with Cristiano Ronaldo and Lionel Messi scoring a goal each from the penalty spot. Four days later, on April 20, they met in a Copa del Rey final, which was a long and tough match. Both teams had their chances, but in the end Real's defense held out against Barça's attack, and Cristiano Ronaldo scored the only goal in extra time.

On April 27, the rivals met again in Madrid in the UEFA Champions League semifinal, and Barça turned things around by winning 2–0. Messi scored both goals late in the match. The second semifinal match was a 1–1 draw in Camp Nou, with Barça going through to the final. The two teams met again in August and played two matches in the Spanish Super Cup (Barça won on away goals), and in December Barcelona won 3–1 in an away match in La Liga. Thus, there were 7 Clásicos in that single year. Barça won 3, Real 1, and 3 ended with a draw.

Pedro
Debuted in 2008
Matches 219
Goals 70
Internationals for Spain 31
Goals 13

Pedro

It's not very common for players to transfer between Barcelona and Real Madrid, as it tends to cause resentment among the supporters of these great rivals. The brilliant Portuguese midfielder Luis Figo found that out when he chose to leave Barça for Real in 2000. Barça's fans had a hard time forgiving him, even though he had given the club five very good years. Bernd Schuster and Michael Laudrup are other players who have taken this same route.

Figo

The most famous player to have gone from Real to Barça was the versatile Luis Enrique. He played for Real Madrid between 1991 and 1996 but then switched sides and turned up at Camp Nou in the blaugrana. He soon won the crowd over and ended up as Barça's skipper. He played a total of 300 matches through 2004 and scored 109 goals.

Luis Enrique

Barcelona held out longer than any other big club against advertising on their jerseys. In 2006, the team broke its long tradition and started playing with the UNICEF logo, although Barça was simply promoting the organization, not receiving money from it. In the summer of 2011, Barcelona made a sponsorship deal with the Qatar Foundation. For the 2013–14 season, the team carries the logo of Qatar Airways.

One of the most celebrated Spanish poets of the 20th century, Rafael Alberti, who was considered a contender for the Nobel Prize, was a strong Barça supporter. He published a famous poem called "Ode to Platkó" after watching the heroic performance of Barça's Hungarian goalkeeper, Ferenc Platkó, in an epic Spanish Cup final against Real Sociedad in 1928. After two draws Barcelona beat Real Sociedad 3–1 to win the cup.

Alberti

Xavi holds the record for the most appearances with Barça. The record was formerly held by the defender Migueli who played a total of 549 matches from 1973 to 1988. He was so devoted and tough that he played in the 1979 Cup Winners' Cup final against Fortuna Düsseldorf with a broken collarbone, even as the match went into extra time.

Lionel Messi now holds the most Barça records when it comes to scoring goals. But even he might have trouble breaking a record set by Lászlo Kubala in La Liga in the 1951–1952 season. In a match against Sporting de Gijón, Kubala scored a whopping total of 7 goals.

Kubala

Learn More!

Books
- Burns, Jimmy. *Barca: A People's Passion.* 2nd ed. London: Bloomsbury, 2009.
- Hunter, Graham. *Barca: The Making of the Greatest Team in the World.* 2nd ed. BackPage Press, 2012.

Websites
- Barcelona maintains website in many languages, fcbarcelona.com, where you can find everything you would want to know about the club and its history, players, games, and results.
- The Wikipedia entry on FC Barcelona also offers an abundance of information about the club.
- espnfc.com (Soccernet)
- goal.com
- 101greatgoals.com
- barcablaugranes.com

Glossary

Striker: A forward player positioned closest to the opposing goal who has the primary role of receiving the ball from teammates and delivering it to the goal.

Winger: The player who keeps to the margins of the field and receives the ball from midfielders or defenders and then sends it forward to the awaiting strikers.

Offensive midfielder: This player is positioned behind the team's forwards and seeks to take the ball through the opposing defense. They either pass to the strikers or attempt a goal themselves. This position is sometimes called "number 10" in reference to the Brazilian genius Pelé, who more or less created this role and wore shirt number 10.

Defensive midfielder: Usually plays in front of his team's defense. The player's central role is to break the offense of the opposing team and deliver the ball to their team's forwards. The contribution of these players is not always obvious but they nevertheless play an important part in the game.

Central midfielder: The role of the central midfielder is divided between offense and defense. The player mainly seeks to secure the center of the field for their team. Box-to-box midfielders are versatile players who possess such strength and foresight that they constantly spring between the penalty areas.

Fullbacks (either left back or right back): Players who defend the sides of the field, near their own goal, but also dash up the field overlapping with wingers in order to lob the ball into the opponent's goal. The fullbacks are sometimes titled wing backs if they are expected to play a bigger role in the offense.

Center backs: These players are the primary defenders of their teams, and are two or three in number depending on formation. The purpose of the center backs is first and foremost to prevent the opponents from scoring and then send the ball towards the center.

Sweeper: The original purpose of the sweeper was to stay behind the defending teammates and "sweep up" the ball if they happened to lose it, but also to take the ball forward. The position of the sweeper has now been replaced by defensive midfielders.

Goalkeeper: Prevents the opponent's goals and is the only player who is allowed to use their hands!

Pick Your Team!

Coach:

_____

Who do you want as Barça's starting eleven? Write the names of the players you want on your team. They don't necessarily have to be real Barça players. And don't forget your coach!

Goalkeeper:

Right back:

Left back:

Defender:

Defender:

Midfielder:

Midfielder:

Midfielder:

Midfielder:

Striker:

Striker:

6

Your striker makes a hole in the goal netting. Wait one round while it's fixed.

8

You establish La Masia. Go forward 3 places!

You win the Copa del Rey for the first time. Go forward 3 places!

Use only one die!

10

You miss out on the title at the last minute. Wait 1 round.

A

B

Barça loses a Clásico. Go to A!

3

12

The Barça Board Game!

Barça wins La Liga for the 1st time. Go forward 1 place.

You get lost in Camp Nou. Go back 3 places.

14

Barcelona founded. Off you go!

C

D

Barça loses in the UEFA Champions League Final. Go to C!

You finally win the Champions League. Go forward 4 places!